# Crumbling Before You

Maholi Díaz

Copyright © 2024 Maholi Díaz

All rights reserved.

ISBN: 9798326851154

Safe Creatives Registration: 2405278108997

Illustrations and cover designed by Maholi Díaz

Crumbling Before *You*

Amiga linda,

Nuestra amistad nació gracias a tu compasión y dulzura. Gracias por tenerme paciencia cuando más lo necesitaba y por TO... tu cariño que significa tanto God, para mi.

family,

friends…

*And every being that brought me pain.*
*It is because of you that I am making my own name.*

Aquí estaré para ti, siempre deseando lo mejor para ti. No sabes lo mucho que me has ayudado ♡ :)

TQM ... jiiijij. xoxo

Just a girl whose heart desired to be loved... beyond words

# CONTENTS

| | |
|---|---|
| Wanting | 7 |
| Silence | 21 |
| Raw | 37 |
| Losing | 56 |
| Healing | 70 |
| Letters to myself | 101 |
| Español | 111 |

Crumbling Before *You*

# WANTING...

## Winter night

The woods bore witness,
to a sublime mist.
Two open hearts,
holding hands while we kissed.

You told me your secrets.
My waist you were holding.
I can't get out of my head,
when I kissed you back…slowly.

The sun was fading…
I found myself glimmering.
I was thinking about you,
even when I was standing next to you.

Our hearts are now closed,
as the winter is over.
We are like wild birds,
free to fly and discover.

The truth is...

I didn't want you to leave.
Let's say…
That winter night was a dream.

Crumbling Before *You*

## Like breathing

Poetry can't be forced.
It needs to flow naturally.
Like the river that goes to the sea.
Poetry, it's your eyes on me.

Like the breath you take,
when we are about to kiss.

## Several miles away

Words flow in a forgotten sea,
waiting for someone to pick them up,
and never let them leave.

If only you knew the words I would like to say…
You would swim away to forever stay...

…with me.

## 365

A poem a day.
A heartless prayer.
Stay with me.
Your laugh, that smile.
In my dreams, you are mine.

Stay with me.

## The saltiness of our efforts

We can walk for miles,
say a thousand lies.
Tonight, we'll be lovers.
We know it leads nowhere.

Thank you for coming,
I've been here waiting.
Now, can we get naked?

I need you tonight.
Tomorrow's another tale.
there's no need to pretend we care.

I drink wine…
Now, your touch drives me wild.
Tonight, we'll be lovers.
We know it leads nowhere.

Crumbling Before *You*

**A candle was lit.**

I could smell your desire.
Your expectation of me.
Between that fire burning our receiving skin.
Your eyes were fixated… staring at me.
Wanting that more,
I wasn't prepared to give.

Gold rings adorning your eyes.
Around a deep blue wanderlust sky.
My heart was beating fast,
but my head is trying for this to last.

Crumbling Before *You*

What do you see when *you close your eyes?*

Same answer for me, each time.

Crumbling Before *You*

**Lie**

Sing to me slowly.
Sing to me and say.
"You are the one who loves me,
I will be right there"

Say the same but twice,
one is not enough.
Write it down in flames.
Brush away the dust.

Help me be the witness.
Feed my pride and lust.
We will be together,
that is now a must.

Hold my hand in laughter.
Hold my hand with pride.
You are the one who loves me.
In my dreams, you are mine.

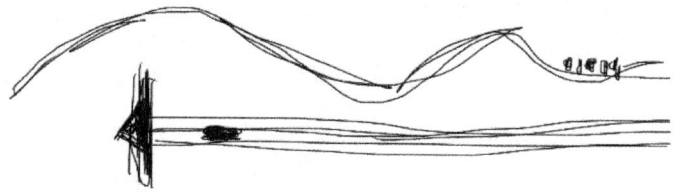

**Lost in desire**

I leave a piece of me,
in every face I look.

Every… body,
my essence proudly took.

Each drags me a bit lower,
to an unrecognisable self.
What I seek seems easy,
but I am hard on myself.

A quest consumes,
and occupies my mind.

Transformed by your presence,
continuously unwind.

## Missing the darkness

A song a day.
A heartless pray.

Your laugh, that smile.
My dream, you are mine.

Lifeless, lonely.

Missing is the only breath I need.
Dark, it's the only home I see.

Would you come and save me?
If you read the words, I keep with me ...

Lifeless, lonely...
Missing the only ...

**Mirror**

Show me light through your eyes.
I will show you mine and never let you leave.
You will notice how I look with them.
You, it's all I see.

## Delusions at night

Just when I thought hope was gone,
I felt it again, so strongly shown.

I never thought I'd see…
But deep down, I know you don't belong to me.
You are so lost.
So fragile. So tossed.

Is it loneliness I recognise?
Or is it just a delusion in disguise?

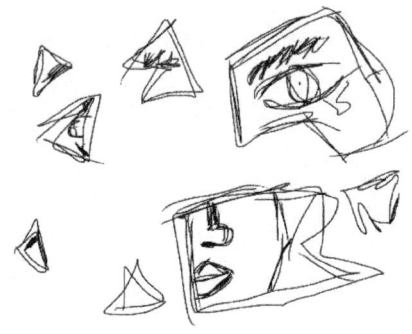

## Timber

What is it about first dates?
that opens a world of possibilities.
A white canvas with no stains.
Making you feel you might find lov*e* again.

That burning desire to touch the lips.
That hoping desire of a perfect kiss.

What is it about first dates,
that we want to know so much,
about a stranger, who desires to be touched.

There is no stranger desire.
To kiss the lips of those you recently admired.
No greater longing than to kiss,
the lips of those we truly miss.

silence...

**It is not easy.**

It is not fair.
It's a war,
a whispered despair.

Being lonely.
Feeling bare.
On an island full of people,
but no one that really cares.

So many hellos.
Too many goodbyes.
How do I tell my soul,
It will continue for a while?

Crumbling Before *You*

**Pouring dry**

It's not about crying anymore,
because there's no sadness to release
Just emptiness to bear.

## The curve I seek

What's more beautiful than the sky?
I repeat this phrase to soothe my mind.
To forget the wear that's hard to swallow.
The world sometimes feels so hollow.

So many faces I see in a day.
Hoping one curves a smile my way.
In their eyes, nothing I perceive.
Empty spaces only love can fill.

I've loved so many times with madness.
A quest for a cure for my sadness.
Does acting "crazy" help in love?
Or is it the reason why it hurts?

## Wearing on me

366 pages I planned.
writing poems every day
the soreness of my arm
It doesn't take the pain away.

So much to say.
So much to do.
So much that wears…

## Silky way

Slowly sinking into my pillow's embrace.
Analysing the image of you, in every trace.

With closed eyes,
I envision you nearby.

If I could only say it.

Crumbling Before *You*

**We hide**

I discover a new world,
in the fresh faces I see.
Just new ways to disguise,
the pain hiding within me.

**Collisions**

I wasn't waiting for your text,
but my heart smiled.
I wasn't expecting to hear from you,
after that last call, you dialled.

I am not expecting a bunch,
and I know that's part of the issue.

I want your love to be sweet,
and not a constant collision.

You like me. Now you don't.
You call me. I don't answer the phone.

You text me: "I miss you…
..don't text me again."
I reply, and we spike again.

In this funny game,
that doesn't have an end.

Crumbling Before *You*

**Twice a day**

The sun touches the roof,
when the sunset hits.

It's beautiful but never long-lasting.

I keep waiting for the next day,
to find that beauty once again.

## All the Time

Sometimes, I miss you.
Sometimes, I am over you.
Sometimes, I want you.

I say "sometimes", but it's *All* the Time

## Glimpse of passion

He knows me better,
he seems to, anyway.
I saw a glimpse of love,
and hold on to that vision for months.

Is she pretty? That you never looked back?
Do you ever think about what we once had?

Your insecure look,
pretending to be Above.
Not letting anyone in,
losing us both.

## Shattered

Planning a future together,
But we didn't even pass leather.

Outside, people saw your best.
I had to settle with more or less.

I didn't voice what you did.
You searched in others,
what you couldn't find within.

The fall was higher than I imagined.
The pieces were smaller than I could gather.

What It "should have been" hunts me.
The person I was, daunts me.

Will I ever be free again?

Crumbling Before *You*

**I see it, I ignore it**

I knew it since I saw your eyes.
That seed of wonder, pain, and desire…

I knew you were looking for someone else to blame.
To pour all the built-up pain.

If I knew the ending,
I'd have done it again.
Loving you wasn't in vain.
Somehow healed my pain and restraint.

## Try

Are you seeking something greater,
thinking you can do better?

You led me to believe I was the one,
only to discover you already had a plus one.

Why do we covet what's not ours to keep?
Knowing it belongs to another's sweep.

Why are we so stubborn,
chasing dreams that are hollow?

Crumbling Before *You*

**C.**

The lines I wrote began with you...
It ended me.

**Learn**

Thinking I was perfect,
made me part of the problem.

I guess healing equals realising.

# RAW...

## Years go by

After a while, it hits you.
Life turned a page.
The old you, the old life,
it has slipped away.
A new path unfolds,
often forced upon.
And oh, you miss it,
that life that's now gone.

You long for the person you used to be.
For the innocence lost, the days carefree.

You miss them dearly,
you want them back.
But deep in your soul,
you know there's a new path.

You've grasped the truth,
it's time to move on.
The mission shifted,
and you've grown.
A new direction,
where everything's rearranged.
The loss of your old self,
a feeling estranged.

Crumbling Before *You*

**Darker the story…**

So many shadows in our path.
Like a mine, if you step on them,
you will be blown to pieces.
The darker the story, the darker the shadow.
Bigger explosion.

**True**

Until a couple of years ago,
I loved being me.
But getting old is tough,
as anyone can see.

I used to adore my reflection's sight.
Thoughts of perfection in my mind now take flight.

I felt the world was mine,
But now my mind can't find the white line.

My thoughts run wild,
with no one to relate.
Escaping my chaos.
A tempting escape.

Crumbling Before *You*

## SASIV

Lying in bed thinking of you.
Like I do,
since the day I got taken away from you.

I feel like time is playing a game.
The one where I am not able to hold your hand again.

This is the way they say it should be.
Unfair as we are clearly meant to be.

You make me love you more every day,
even though we are 1000 miles away.

## Strangers

A girl wanders the city streets.
A heart full of nostalgia loudly beats.
A camera flash catches her eye,
no more to touch her soul, so shy.

She realises he's capturing her, just as she is.
In her rawness, her truth, her personal abyss.

Through his lens, she finds her bliss,
she feels the warmth of a soul's first kiss.

## Loving, losing

Corroding to the bone.
Feeling my heart alone.
All the trust I had.
Went away in the blink of an eye.

Do I even respect you anymore?
Do I even respect myself for opening my heart?
What should I do? I wonder...
What should I think? I ponder.

Why did you act this way?
Proving that men are all built the same way.

I wish I could be where I was a year ago.
I'd have the dream and my eyes would be shut.

How do I move on after this?
I feel so alone I can't breathe.

## Freedom?

I found myself,
looking for poems about divorce.
Looking for someone,
who has experienced the Beyond.

Described the pain eloquently,
like if it didn't hurt suddenly.

I want to leave behind,
that copper shield on my soul,
built of a broken heart.

Today, I am officially divorced.
One day, I will be completely free.

*My favourite stage of grief is denial.*

Crumbling Before *You*

## Wearing masks

Happy faces and random places.
Silly conversation.
No deep connections.
I want to stay present,
but few talks are pleasant.

There's so much I can pretend,
to keep my feelings at bay.
So much pain to put away,
for a few hours of relay.

If I keep myself alone,
I feel peace and reborn.

If I keep myself alone,
I can avoid the mistakes I'm hunted for.

If I keep myself alone,
the wall grows wider,
and I feel protected.
But the problem with that feeling is ….
Your soul isn't detected.

You get lost and forgotten,
and your connections begin too rotten.

How do I do when friendships demand attention,
but my soul seeks disconnection?
Should I listen to my soul?
Or try another day, once more?

## Poetry

Most poetry,
beautiful yet untidy.
Deeply flawed.
Grammatically incorrect,
like life's own dialect.

Doesn't always make sense.
A soft game of pretend,
a constant test.

But through it all,
we must be brave.
Facing each twist with faith.

# Crumbling Before *You*

**Love is my name.**

Desire is your game.
Hope is your aim.
Lust is your escape.
Happiness is your will.
Pride is your fear.

# Crumbling Before *You*

*Why do we call "real one" to the love that breaks our hearts the most?*

## Scripts to failure

Are you as confused as I am?
About this game, they call love.
When you want to get closer,
It's on me to say no.
It's a game we can't take command of.

The song we never heard before.
But we both know every word to the core.

## Scars

To find me again, I need to dig deep.
Deep in the cuts I have in my skin.
Clear the bruises of an eaten-up heart,
mitigate the desire to fall apart.

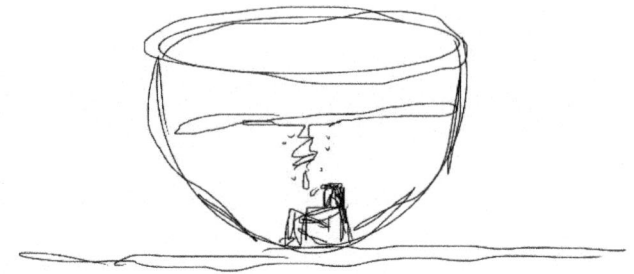

**Tearless**

I feel I want to cry.
But tears don't flow.
My body is telling me,
"You need to stop".

# Crumbling Before *You*

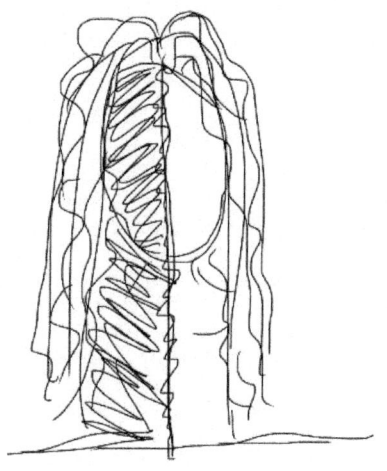

*The human mind is an anticipation machine.*

**Cry while trying**

I don't cry after a breakup,
because I cry myself to sleep while trying.
After enough disappointment, my tears dry.

Crumbling Before *You*

**We know**

Are we really surprised when love fails?
Or do we see the signs? but pretend they are not there?

We choose blindness over objectivity.
Playing games with our vulnerability.

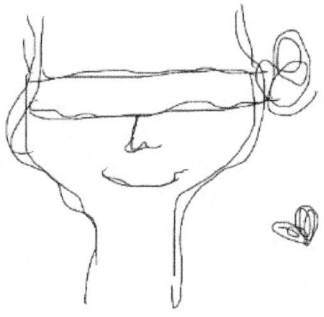

losing…

## Back to black

I heard the plans.
You moved on, and I...
keep pretending. I am smiling.

Did you... did I ... did we....?
I did. I thought we were meant to be.

Nothing feels to hold.
The time is moving slowly..., and I,
keep pretending. I am shining.

You took a piece...
Of the messed-up dream.
That is to have a happy ending.

I am back in the dark.
I can't pretend any more.
It's there for everyone to know.
Not the fairytale I imagined.

I can't pretend any more.
It's there for everyone to know.
I wrote you an "I hate you" poem.

## Do I?

I want to stop searching,
for your face in the crowd.
I want to stop seeking,
your scent all around.

## Why

It's impossible you haven't thought about me.

Right?...

Why do I need confirmation?
It's my ego that desires your attention.

My heart wants to be free from oppression.

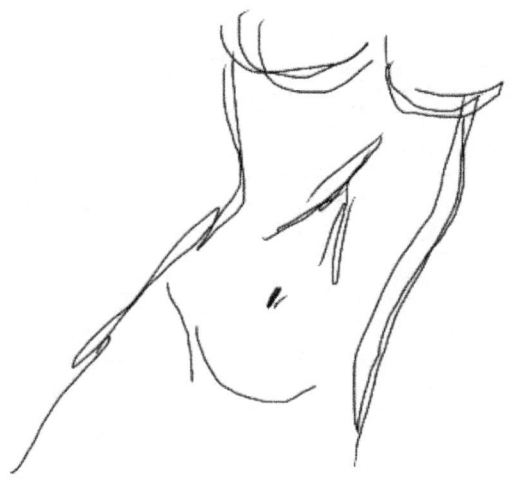

**Losing you**

I have a hole in my soul,
where our friendship used to be.

## Again, I knew

The heart can really break.
The boy who walked away,
after chasing me for years.

I knew it all along.
You are not where I belonged.
When you saw I was awake,
and that jump I was willing to take.

You packed and walked away.

**Hoping**

Maybe mentioning your name,
will bring you back.
Maybe loving you,
is only about what I lack.

Crumbling Before *You*

## Brief pleasure

I haven't allowed myself to feel grief,
as anger has been on the surface.
Darkness, sorrow.
Marks and bruises.

The understanding,
that my place next to you,
was supposed to be brief.
Burns, scars, but it also relieves.

Sadness takes over,
and realisation takes place.
A life without the other,
profound scars won't be erased.

**Running wild**

Millions of thoughts,
floating with no control.
How do I stop, though?
This feeling of "knowing" it was you.

## Rules

I am wounded.
Like never before.
Healing seems impossible,
when the time has gone.

Love was the promise,
betrayal was your rule.
Always making others,
playthings in your pool.

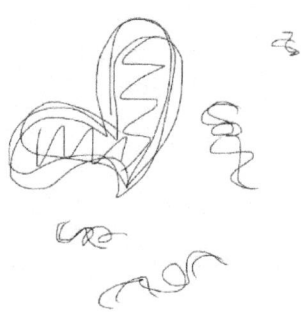

## Forbidden words

It could have been me,
but you looked away.
It could have been me,
but I was always afraid.

I pretend I'm strong.
I pretend I'm not wrong.
Showing love by faith.
Vulnerability is not my best trait.

I look for you in every face,
I think God will put you on my path once again.

## Crumbling Before *You*

*Sometimes I can't find the right words to say…*

*I need to write a poem instead.*

## Da capo

Wrong time to kiss.
Wrong time to take.
The right time to miss.

Maybe if I write it again,
I will believe it myself…
that I don't want to see you again.

Sometimes, it is not the right time.

Wrong time to kiss,
Wrong time to take,
The right time to miss.

*Sometimes, it is not the right find.*

## November rain

A white Christmas tree,
already in my view.
People are passing by,
I am looking out for you.
You are not even close by,
but I still crave for you.

Thinking of you every minute of the day,
hoping this feeling finally goes away.

healing...

## Beneath the Surface

Digging deep sounds scary,
more when all your life…
your feelings have been buried.

So many people took advantage of you…
but deep down, you already knew.

Why did you ignore all the signs? I wonder…
Choosing the direct path to rain and thunder?

Ego, pride? All the wrong reasons.
Finding love that only lasts a season.

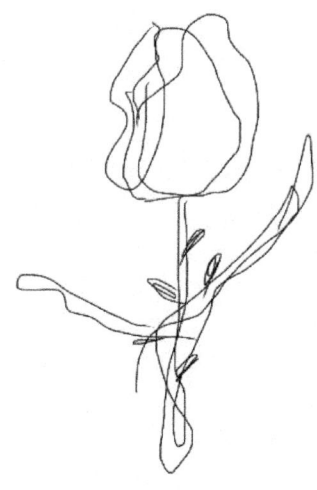

**Goodbye home**

Wondering how we ended up where we are is a constant.

Questioning if our decisions are the best is permanent.

Trusting ourselves is essential.
Relying on God to guide us is imminent.

*...At least, that's what I say to myself.*

Crumbling Before *You*

**Repeat every day**

Let the tears run.
Let the sadness come.
Let the memories flow.
As the heart grows.

Let that new place.
Be the new way.
For your soul to heal…
Happy tears will finally appear.

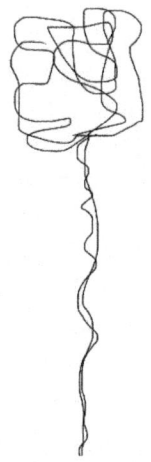

## Live

I now, live my life on the edge.
Don't be jealous.
Heal the same.

## Ocean view

Feeling the sand on my feet.
Looking forward and realising,
that even from afar…
We are still connected with the horizon.

## Opening my heart

Letting the darkness go,
by sharing my deepest fears.
Finding comfort in the pain,
of letting you see my tears.

They poured and cleaned my soul,
making me feel fulfilled.
What is it about friendships,
that shows love is real.

## Me First

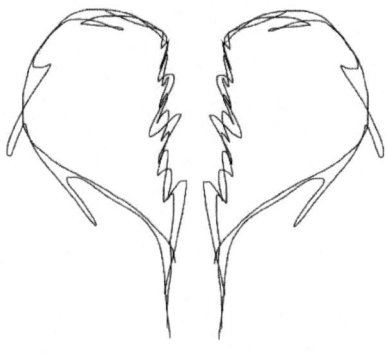

**Awake**

My eyes were too shut for me to see,
all the opportunities I had in front of me.
All the experiences I was leaving behind.
I focused more on what I lacked.

Tonight, I am digging deep into my soul.
For the pain to come to the surface.
I want my soul to resurface.

Understanding ourselves takes a while.
We go through so much pain.
Building who we are out of the fire.
We burn often, but ashes can be rebuilt.
Our souls are stronger than we might think.

Crumbling Before *You*

*Rely on connections to survive.*

**Humanity**

The person before you has scars.
She needs to find peace in her own time.

We break the pattern of self-destruction.
By looking at ourselves, with patience and devotion.

There is no one to blame.
We all have traumas.
Now I call friend,
who I used to call Mama.

**Be light.**

The light of our soul reflects in our actions.

**Take control**

The good thing about life,
is that it's unpredictable.

But if you know what you want from it,
life becomes a spectator more than a guide.

## Captures

Sometimes, we don't realise that a picture is a magical tool.

It allows us to do what we don't do often.

Stop for a second and look closer.

## Chase the rain

Chase the sun.
Chase a breeze.
In early June.

Free the pain.
Watch the moon.
Open your eyes,
for infinite youth…

Be yourself and rest assured…

If you do this, you will see clear blue.

## Soul, mates

Sometimes, you connect with people on another level.

They might not even be in your life anymore,
but that universal connection will stay there forever to
remember that we are not alone in the world.

We belong to infinite souls.

Some stay forever.

## Feelings of peace

This year is about digging deep in my soul,
I want to find out who I am,
and try to make myself whole.
Deconstructing my being, layer by layer.
Answering the questions, I've long held in prayer.

It's maturing, it's learning, it's feeling the pain.
Allowing myself to suffer, to grow from the strain.
Lessons condensed in a fast-track recovery,
like the burn before the phoenix's discovery.

What a stage in life, to feel so lost!
A necessary journey, no matter the cost.
My advice: seek help in every possible way.
For in asking for guidance, you'll find your own say.

Crumbling Before *You*

**Asking for help was a struggle.**

Letting someone in,
lose control and just give in.
My pride. Itch.
My desire for control. Glitch.

I have been let down before,
when it wasn't much I was asking for.

That disappointment sticks in my soul.
Makes me rebuild all my high walls.

True friendships and kind hearts,
take the canvas and make it art.

I was holding my breath,
but now I can breathe,
knowing that someone will be there for me.

Genuine, unintentional.
With just the desire,
to curve my face,
with a bright smile.

## Divine changes

Her skin was different.
Her wrinkles were deeper.
But she stood so tall,
that my eyes just admired her.

And without her knowing:
she created a core memory in me.
Is not about age.
And she proved it to me.

The time showed in her skin with no mercy.
And me, looking at myself so gently.

#selflove

# Crumbling Before *You*

**I sabotage.**

I hate.
I deny.
I regret.
I question the existence.
And I ask,
Why is the pain so persistent?

I confide.
I love.
I lose control.
I speak Above.
I think many times,
Why does it burn to my core?

I destroy.
I rebuild.
I construct.
I re-think.

It's exhausting.
But I do it
There's no other way.
I knew it…

**Thank you**

I found peace in my friends.
Someone willing to listen.
Someone willing to stay.
Even if the story has been told,
One thousand times again.

You. Who I never met before.
You stayed with me.
Tried to heal my broken heart.
We all suffer and are full of stories.
Life is laugh, loss and worries.

If you are lucky enough.
to find light in your life.
Treat them the same and stick for a while.

Crumbling Before *You*

**Enough about hate**

I really want to be free.
I want to heal the bruise,
that is deep down inside me.
I want to think about coffee when I open my eyes.
Anything apart from the pain,
that disturbs my mind.

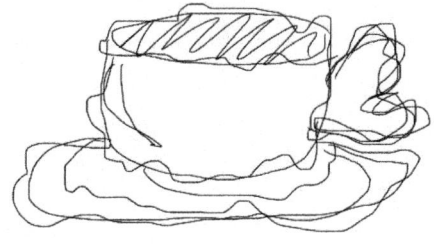

Crumbling Before *You*

**Find me again**

Lights hanging from the ceiling.
A Christmas tree hugging a homey feeling.
I sit by myself, thinking of You.
A man I don't know,
but I give my heart to.

Couples walk by,
holding hands tight.
Laughing or fighting,
their hearts align.
Should I be grateful,
with nothing to mourn?

I am alive, healthy, and waiting for dawn.

I know You find me, somehow, some way.

In this world of wonders, come what may.

## Smiling

Writing about heartbreak. Nothing better to it.

It's the chaos I enjoy.
Sometimes, it can fill the void.

It was in my nature to enjoy the pain.
Now, I know better. I will be happy again.

## Micro breaks

There is no real cure more than time,
to fix the shadows, we try to hide.

Tiny particles of loss and grief.
Those unfulfilled places we dearly miss.

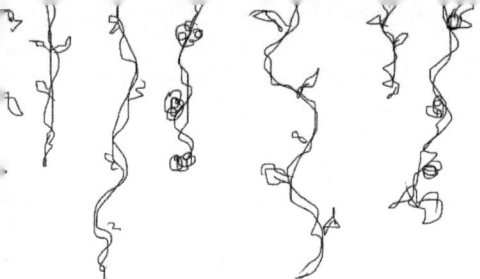

Crumbling Before *You*

**Flowers, dates, kisses, poems.**

It is so romantic to speak about love.
In this life, we also have loss.
Pain and gain as the song goes.

Dreams, flowers, talks.
Makes me think of all the love I lost.
Let's not forget. All friendships I gain.
Especially with myself.

**Your Colours**

I opened my heavy eyes.
And now wonder…
How does the soft golden kiss your curves?
…And I smile
Like if it was the first time.

A deep dark green,
adorning both of your sides.
And in the middle…
your narrow lines.

I have seen your colours a thousand times,
but you still dazzled me, and I smile…
again like it's the first time.

I speak to God thanks to you.

What is it about country roads,
that makes me think of You?

Crumbling Before *You*

**Scotland**

Understand the beauty of your flag,
by looking at the almost clear blue sky.

Blue, white and peace.
There is still so much I miss...
This is the place I now belong.
 I left home so many moons ago.

I hold my breath and thank you again.

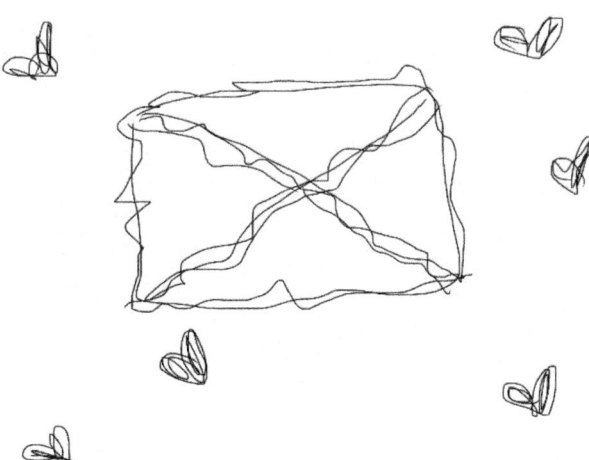

## Breathing

We need to be aware.
Not everyone is the same.
Some people give,
Some people take.
Some are forever there.

Some give you peace,
Some provide you with despair.
Some souls are meant to give you…

A breath of fresh air.

Crumbling Before *You*

**Near the end**

Do you have to stop yourself from doing things you really want to do... ?

How do you feel after?

Have you ever managed to have a real conversation with anyone?

Deep, open, powerful?

Have you cried in front of a friend?

Do you pressure yourself to be the ideal person everyone thinks you should be?

How many times did you change what you were going to say in the first place?


Who would you say for sure, that loves who you are?

Do you believe in love?

Would you read what a stranger sent?

Would you give it a thought?
Would you reply, or would you stop yourself again?
To be honest, I don't need you to reply.

It would be good just to know you read this.

Has anyone asked you questions?

About you, about your soul.

## Crumbling Before *You*

Who are you?

Do you even have one, a soul?

I wish we could live in a poem.

However, poems are even changed to be liked by others.

So, this is me. Not changing my last poem.

# Letters to myself

## When I feel ugly

When you question your beauty, just come back to the basics. Wash off the makeup, wear comfortable clothes, and look at yourself in a mirror, but look at yourself with love and embrace. YOU as you are.

The best person to tell you - you are beautiful - is yourself; what a great feeling.

No one will ever change your mind if you believe it. We are lovely, and we can improve. Love yourself and love the man who loves you.

I know you feel lost sometimes and not worthy, but at some point, you need to understand that you will never be able to be someone else but yourself.

Your skin, your hair, your eyes, your eyelashes. They will be yours forever.

We can treat them, dye them, curl them, or try to shape our bodies into something different, but our essence will be there, wanting to come out eventually.

**When I try to understand m*e***

Writing gives me oxygen.
If I don't write, I risk soul contamination.
It would hold contradictions.
My addictions, my sadness.
Are all released into the unknown?
Depurate my soul.
Hoping they will all stop.
Or at least take the pain to dust.

## When I don't like myself

You have an internal richness seen before.
Empathic, you want others to feel more.

You craft a welcoming home, both for you and others.
Building it yourself, with hands that make it grander.
Strong emotions, a mind so rich.
Capable of taking one step beyond, a bewitch.

Our thoughts are just that, not who we truly are,
In the depths of our souls, we find our true star.

# Crumbling Before *You*

**When I look for the one**

Finding the love in my parents
Finding the love in my friends
Finding the love in myself

*Everything* is meaningful, it's just new to your eyes.

# Crumbling Before *You*

My *love runs out* if not watered

Crumbling Before *You*

If I could see *what others see*, I might think highly about "me".

## My best friend just told me:

*Here you are thinking about him. He is probably thinking of how to make money.*

I laughed.

**Aquarius and Pisces**

Living in dreams is addictive.
Your mind weaves the story,
imaginative and descriptive.

# Españo*l*...

Algunos poemas y pensamientos...

deben conservar su esencia original.

No hay posible traducción.

Gracias por leer.

## Párpados pesados cual acero.

Venas en mis ojos delatan mis pensamientos.
Párpados tan pesados cual acero,
no consigo conciliar el sueño.

Una paz mental que no existe,
no me deja descansar.
Muchas cosas en qué pensar.

Mis ojos engañarían que yo dormía,
remolinos número cinco se llevan el sueño.

Traen insomnio arraigado, adolorido y acumulado.

No dejo de pensarte, extrañarte y quererte.
Anhelo el privilegio de abrazarte nuevamente.
Pronto nos veremos otra vez.

Voy cayendo en la oscuridad finalmente.
Allí... es cuando toco tu mano y siento que no ha sido en vano.

Me respondes *"mi amor adorado,*
*he estado pensando en ti,*
*espero algún día puedas ser feliz sin mí.*
*Ya hace un tiempo te he dejado,*
*para unirme a un plan más sagrado.*
*Espero entiendas siempre te amaré*
*y desde los cielos yo te cuidaré."*

Despierto y no estás a mi lado. Sueños de oro.

Esperar por ellos es tortura, pero lo haría cada noche sin duda. Unidos estaremos otra vez.

*Sentarse* a la orilla de la playa.
Mirar al frente y entender... que aún en la lejanía...
estás conectado con el horizonte.

## Crumbling Before *You*

*Amarte* es un delirio constante,
tratando de no mirarte fijamente.
Pero azul es mi color favorito,
y tus ojos de color "hogar" resplandeciente.

## Crumbling Before *You*

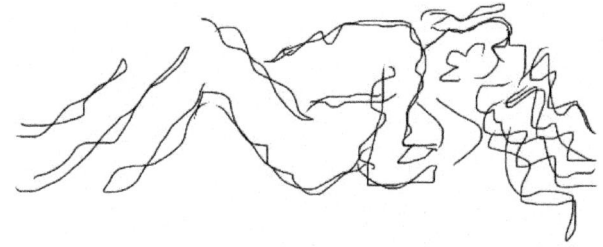

*¿Cuántas veces debo besar la pantalla para que aparezcas?*

**Pensar**

Eso es lo bueno de la vida.
Impredecible como ella sola.
Pero si sabes lo que quieres,
ella se convierte en espectadora en vez de guía.

Este *amor* va más allá de las fronteras.
Transciende en el tiempo y no sabe de barreras.

**Patrones**

Somos reflejo de la naturaleza
y en nosotros se repite su ciclo.
Aunque sea imperceptible,
la vida tiene un latido silencioso
Debemos verla con ojos curiosos.

# Crumbling Before *You*

*Tienes un gran corazón e infinitas bendiciones*

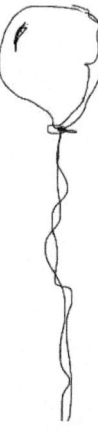

## *A*-Dios

Sentir un espacio vacío se ha vuelto hábito,
pero en días especiales se vuelve más profundo.

Como si un puño presionara mi pecho.

Y es mi propio puño.

No siento dolor. Solo vacío.
El vacío duele. Si eso tiene sentido.

Trato de controlar mis sentimientos, como siempre, y
parar de recordar ciertos momentos.

Como la última vez que las vi y dije…

"nos vemos luego".

## Carmen

Cuando te miran y realmente se alegran de verte, se nota en la mirada.

Indescriptible cuando esos ojitos se hacían chiquitos por la sonrisa interna que emanabas.

Ojitos oscuros con azul llenos de amor interminable.


Me pasaba contigo cada vez.

*La luz de tu alma se refleja en tus acciones. Sé brillante.*

# Crumbling Before *You*

**Ecos**

A veces no reconozco la persona que era antes, en mi niñez y adolescencia. Siento que me cuentan la historia de alguien más porque muchas cosas no las haría y muchas más… las valoraría.

*Extrañarlas es "normal" pero no saber cuándo diré otra vez "Hola ya llegué" ... es ... mortal.*

La *curvatura* de tu sonrisa no denota tristeza o felicidad. Es el resultado de tu esfuerzo frente a la adversidad.

## No pensar

Pensar en ti,
es un hábito constante,
con repetición fehaciente.

Pensar en ti,
es un trabajo a tiempo completo,
realizado diariamente,
con remuneración inmediata,
de pensarte nuevamente.

Unos ojos color mar,
con matiz de inmensidad.
Cuando cierro los ojos,
no puedo ver algo más.

Pensar en ti es delirio y tortura,
mezclada con amor y ternura.

Unos labios que no puedo besar,
pero jamás dejaré de desear.

Espero el día que no tenga que pensar,
sino verte fijamente, finalmente.

## Mañan*a*

A veces no quiero dormir porque le temo al *mañana*

Sé que va a doler.
Es como repetir la misma historia una y otra vez

Tanto dolor.
Tanta soledad.
Tanto vacío.
¿Dónde está felicidad?

No envidio a quien la encuentra.
Rezo que tu felicidad crezca.

Evaluó la mía y me pregunto si soy el problema

¿Qué hago aquí?
¿Cómo llegue a dónde estoy?
¿Por qué pienso así?

No sé ni quién soy.
No sé qué camino tomar.

Estoy perdida,
y solo consigo romper.

¿Qué quieres de mí?
¿Hasta dónde me vas a llevar?
A este punto de no retorno
¿Cuál es la lección que debo enfrentar?

La *perseverancia* es un amigo de la dificultad cuando el destino gobierna el juego.

## Loca

Miro a la distancia y encuentro consuelo.
"¿Qué más bonito que admirar el cielo?"

Me repito a mí misma esa última frase.
Para olvidar lo incrustado de mi desgaste.

El mundo a veces parece desierto.
Sin el hada que debería tener el cuento.

Tantos rostros miro en un día,
con la esperanza de que uno sonría.

Nada percibo en ellos.
Parecen buscar el mismo consuelo.
Vacíos, que el amor sólo sabe llenar.
Aunque, a mí, no me ha podido encontrar.

He amado tantas veces con locura.
Un esfuerzo al que le busco cura.
¿Actuar "loco" ayuda en el amor?
¿O solo marchita el corazón y la razón?

# Crumbling Before *You*

Esta *vida* es una ilusión pasajera

**Odiarte nunca.**

Lánzame una mirada hostil de esas que queman el alma; porque aún si me odias, sabré que me miras.
Lánzame una mirada hostil y fulmíname como haces en sueños; aún si me odias, sabré que me miras.

Conéctate conmigo un segundo. Si luego tus párpados arden y tus ojos quedan en blanco, aún sabré que me miras.

Soy el único capaz de volver tu odio en risa.

Al mirarme, serás mía.

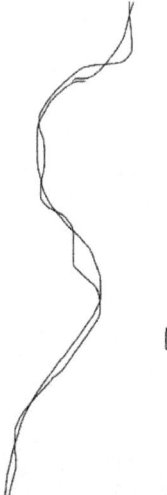

Si el empuje hacia la luz no estuviera ya latente en el germen escondido en la tierra, *el loto* jamás tendería hacia la luz...

# Crumbling Before *You*

En algún momento e instante en el tiempo pensaré en ti.

No a cada minuto, como ahora, pero pensaré en ti…

*Recordaré un amante* que siempre estuvo distante y un corazón ausente…

Cuento las horas para que el mañana venga y pueda dejar de verte …

Tiempo es lo que necesito para olvidarte, pero tiempo es lo que más tengo para pensarte.

Quiero dejar de soñarte ahorita, cuando mi alma arde y mi corazón palpita…

Por ahora, sigo pensándote.

***Te amo*** más de lo que las palabras expresan y te extraño más que lo que el corazón puede soportar.

La esperanza es un arma de doble filo que viene y va a su hartar.

# Crumbling Before *You*

Hoy desperté con unas ***ganas sublimes*** de leer poesía.

De esas, que expresan los deseos ocultos debajo de nuestra fachada de lo que "debemos" ser.

De esas que te dan una sensación inexplicable de conexión con tu alma y espíritu al leerlas.

Algo así como colocarte un pañito tibio sobre el rostro para que broten todas las impurezas. De esas. . .

## Distancia

La distancia es forzada.
Nadie quiere decir 'estoy lejos' de lo que quiere.
La distancia es como comerse un limón sin diluirlo en agua.
Amargo, pero que terminas pasando y creyendo que te acostumbraste.

Hasta la segunda mordida.

Ahí, vuelves a arrugar la cara del ardor...

# Crumbling Before *You*

**En tu felicidad encuentro la mía.**

Mirándome como un reflejo de vida.
Si tan solo una lágrima se llega a formar,
en tus ojos, esos que deseo ver brillar…

Quiero decirte que duele
Y duele más que mi pesar.
Sin ti no sabría qué hacer, qué creer. o saber cómo renacer.

Sin tu apoyo no sería nada, sin tu ejemplo estaría todavía acorralada.
Me has enseñado a creer, a vivir, a soñar y querer.

Un amor tan puro que me hace respirar, en un mundo que a veces puede sofocar.
Solo tu felicidad quiero ver y tu ser, ver florecer.
La vida es frágil y puede tirarte rocas.
Amistad como esta he tenido pocas.
Gracias por estar para mí.
Si un día mi espalda llegas a herir,
moriría feliz…sabiendo que estuviste allí para mi…

Tantos años cuidando de mí.

## Dime

Estoy asustada,
de no lograr lo que me propongo.
De quedarme estancada.

De perder mis años de cordura,
y perder la razón por pesimismo.

La persona que era siento que ya no está…
y que tengo una sombra de lo que era.

Me siento desconectada conmigo un poco con Dios y lo que debería estar haciendo.
¿Cómo se encuentra el camino de vuelta?

Luego leo…

*Deja correr las lágrimas*
*Deja que venga la tristeza*
*Deja fluir los recuerdos*
*A medida que crece el corazón*
*Deja que ese nuevo lugar*
*Sea la nueva forma de admirar*
*Tu alma sanará*
*Y las lágrimas de felicidad, finalmente, aparecerán.*

## Crumbling Before *You*

*No sé cómo nos encontramos ... pero los rayos de sol que emites...calientan un invierno interminable*

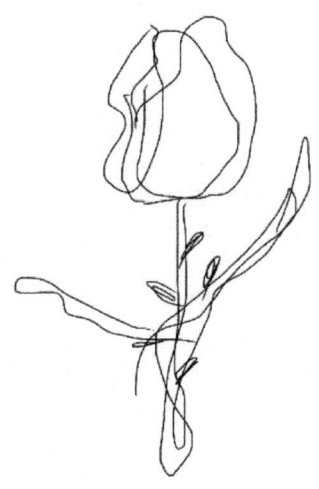

## ABOUT THE AUTHOR

Maholi *Díaz* was born in Caracas, Venezuela, a vibrant city that cultivated her love for chaos, passion, poetry, and art.

At 26, she moved to Scotland, leaving family and friends behind. She lived in a constant quest for love, beauty, and pain. A journey that brought sunshine, storm, and strain.

Maholi's journey of healing and self-discovery is ongoing after facing heartbreak, divorce, therapy, and identity loss. She now stands *tall*.

Printed in Great Britain
by Amazon